Facts Of The Visit To Boyle Of The Fathers Rinolfi & Lockhart, Missioners Of The Church Of Rome

in the effort to meet this special Mission against the preaching of the Gospel to Roman Catholics.. The following Challenge was sent to the Rev. Messrs. Rinolfi and Lockhart:—

Boyle, May 26, 1853.

REVEREND GENTLEMEN,—Having seen it publicly announced that you are about to open a Roman Catholic Mission in the town of Boyle, we, the undersigned Ministers of the Church of Ireland, desire respectfully to lay before you the following proposition, in the hope that you may be led to regard a compliance with it as adapted to advance an object which ought to fill the foremost place in the heart of every Minister of Christ;—the firmer establishment and the more extended diffusion of truth.

The differences between the Churches of Rome and Ireland are neither few nor unimportant, but concern so intimately the leading articles of the Christian's faith, that both cannot by any possibility be regarded as equally safe and right.

We are sure you will agree with us, that it would be not only lamentable blindness as to facts, but a course totally opposed to the principles of the two churches in question, to permit an impression to prevail, that men with equal safety to their souls might indifferently profess one or other of these opposite creeds.

We would therefore respectfully invite you to a PUBLIC CONFERENCE upon the differences between the Churches of Rome and Ireland. If you are disposed to oppose three or more articles from the creed of the Church of Ireland, we are ready to undertake their defence; upon the terms that we shall be permitted to oppose, and that you shall defend a similar number of articles from the creed of Pope Pius the IV.

We shall wait upon you to settle the requisite preliminaries for this conference as soon as you may be at leisure to do so.

If you should prefer a discussion through the medium of the public press, we are authorized to state that the requisite space will be granted by the proprietor of the local newspaper, to both parties, for this purpose.

We have the fullest and most unhesitating faith in the strength and power of truth, however feebly it may be maintained, and however ably it may be resisted. For a time it may seem to be overborne, but it never can be vanquished finally because it is the cause of God. It may have its dwelling place in the heart of but one man, and yet will he prove stronger than the whole world beside; and though he may not live to see it, his principles will eventually triumph. Hence truth has at all times been characterized by its fearlessness, and resolute facing of opposition; while error has ever been distrustful, and shrinking, as if sensible of its own weakness.

6

We need hardly remind you that in the early ages of the Church the Apostles and their immediate followers were always ready to meet their antagonists, and convince them by reasoning.

Such especially was the conduct of St. Paul, as described in Acts xvii, 2,—" Secundum consuetudinem autem Paulus introivit ad eos et per sabbata tria disserebat eis de Scripturis."—Vulgate. ("And Paul according to his custom went in unto them: and for three Sabbath-days he reasoned with them out of the Scriptures." Douay Version.)

He also in his Epistle to Titus I, 9, lays down the following rule for every minister of the Word of God—" Amplectentem eum qui secundum doctrinam est fidelem sermonem : ut potens sit exhortari in doctrina sana, *et eos qui contradicunt, arguere.*"— Vulgate. (" Embracing that faithful word which is according to doctrine, that he may be able to exhort in sound doctrine, and to *convince the gainsayers.*"—Douay Version.

Sanctioned by such authority, we trust that the coarse which we invite you to pursue, will not be regarded as inexpedient or inconsistent with your position as Ministers of Christ.

We are, Reverend Gentlemen,
Your very humble servants,

JOHN M. MAGUIRE,
Vicar of Boyle, &c. ;

GEO. W. DALTON,
Missionary to Roman Catholics and Vicar of Kilbryan.

Rev. Messrs. RINOLFI and LOCKHART.

The following invitation also was sent to the Rev. W. Lockhart :—

Boyle, May 26, 1853.
REVEREND SIR,—You come to Boyle on a " Mission,"—I also have come to Boyle on a " Mission" ;—

You subscribed at your Matriculation at Oxford to the 39 Articles of Religion ; I also at my ordination at Oxford subscribed to them ;—

We are here both engaged in *similar* labours—and we both once subscribed to the *same* articles of Religion ;—

When in Oxford, you believed that " The Romish doctrine concerning Purgatory, Pardons, Worshipping, and Adoration, as well of Images as of Reliques, and also Invocations of Saints is a fond thing vainly invented, and grounded upon *no warranty* of Scripture, but rather repugnant to the Word of God."—Article xxii.

Now in Boyle you " steadfastly hold that there is a Purgatory —that the Saints are to be honored and invocated—and most firmly assert that the Images of Christ and also of the Saints may be had and retained, and that due honor and veneration are to be given to them."—Creed Pius IV,—Art 7, 8, 9.

When in Oxford you believed "Those *five* commonly called Sacraments, that is to say, Confirmation, Penance, Orders, Matrimony, Extreme Unction are not to be counted for Sacraments of the Gospel, for that they have not any visible sign or ceremonial ordained of God."—Article xxv.

Now in Boyle you "profess that there *are* truly and properly *Seven* Sacraments of the New Law instituted by Jesus Christ our Lord."—Creed Pius IV,—Art 3.

When in Oxford you declared by your Subscription that "Transubstantiation in the Supper of the Lord, *cannot be proved* by Holy Writ, but is repugnant to the plain words of Scripture, and overthroweth the nature of a Sacrament."—Art. xxviii.

Now in Boyle you "profess that there *is* made a conversion of the whole substance of the Bread into the Body and of the whole substance of the Wine into the Blood—called Transubstantiation."—Creed, Pius IV—Art. 5.

You thus *now deny*, what *once* you *believed*!

I *still* believe what I then believed;—

You must either have or not have *reasons* for *such* a change of mind!

If the Truth is *now* believed by you, it can persuade me also and all who may hear it at your lips;—

I invite you therefore to a Public Meeting at any time and place most convenient to yourself, where you shall have every opportunity to give the reasons why you have changed, and I shall give the reasons why I have not changed from the belief in what we once equally professed.

He who really has discovered and possesses the Truth will be the readiest to communicate it and the reasons for its acceptance to others.

Awaiting your reply I am, Rev. Sir,
Yours faithfully,
GEO. W. DALTON, A.B.,
Missionary to Roman Catholics and Vicar of Kilbryan.

Mr. Rinolfi arrived alone and commenced the effort of Rome, on the 26th of May, by an introductory Sermon lauding the supposed blessings of this Mission, and denouncing in sweeping terms the Proselytizing movement, agents and converts. In the course of his harangue he was understood by all present to defy the Missionaries to come forward and defend their Ordination. The following note, accepting his Challenge, was immediately sent to the residence of the Priest:—

Boyle, May 26, 1853.

REVEREND SIR,—You are reported to have said in your address in Boyle Chapel this morning that you did "Defy the Missionaries to come forward and prove their Ordination further back than the time of Henry VIII—consequently that they had no commission from Christ."

You asserted the same respecting our Ordination as Protestant Clergymen, this evening, when we were permitted to hear you.—

Now, Reverend Sir, We *at once* accept your challenge! and have to request of you to name any day and place when WE will "*come forward* and *prove* that *our* ordination" is direct and unbroken from the ANCIENT IRISH CHURCH; and, consequently, that WE, and NOT YOU, are rightly commissioned, and are successors of St. Patrick, the Apostle of Ireland.

We presume that you will not shrink from the Challenge you have put forth so publicly!

Awaiting your reply, we are, Rev. Sir,
Yours faithfully,

W. C. TOWNSEND,
Missionary to Roman Catholics;

GEO. W. DALTON,
Missionary to Roman Catholics and Vicar of Kilbryan;

JOHN M. MAGUIRE,
Vicar of Boyle, &c.

Rev. Mr. RINOLFI, R.C.C.

This note was returned unopened with the message that, Mr. Rinolfi would hold no communication with the writers of it. It was then sent to him thro' the Post, and a copy was forwarded to the local Paper. At the same time a fresh placard was issued, asking the reason why the Mission Fathers defied the Missionaries and then shrunk from them when they accepted the Challenge put forth—were they afraid of their own Bible in a discussion.

During the stay of Mr. Rinolfi two important Sermons were preached by the Vicar of Boyle; one upon Transubstantiation, and the other upon the Perversions which occurred from the Church of England, and the Desire for Reformation which was manifested on the Continent.

The attendance of Protestants at the Evening Meetings was very good—manifesting an increasing interest in becoming acquainted with the reasons for the differences between the two Churches. It now became apparent that the Mission Fathers dreaded Discussion and Controversy as much as the Priests themselves, and disappointment was felt by many of the Roman Catholics. The Host was for the first time here exposed for Adoration for forty hours. Confessions were carried on daily. Every engine was brought to bear to check the missionary work here.— Language most exciting in its nature was fully indulged in by Mr. Rinolfi. But a stronger than he restrained the violence of the ignorant people.

Mr. Rinolfi left the town amidst the triumphant shouts of the rabble,—having failed to shake the hold the Scriptures have obtained in the hearts of one or two individuals, altho' he personally visited in one case, and fulminated tearful woe against all Jumpers, Bible Readers, and those who lodged the Scripture Readers. In one case the Priests paid into a Servant's hand Five Shillings to induce her to leave her Mistress, and no longer to cook for " devils," as they termed the Readers. To the honor of those who had Readers lodging with them, we must add, they were firm, and refused to eject the Readers.

The Sermon advertised for the 5th of June was postponed. On the 17th Mr. Lockhart arrived—followed and proceeded by a mob, yelling forth their cheers and delight. Expectation never was so aroused. Here was a man from a great University converted to Romanism. Now, if ever, would Rome see her Champion, and the People expected that now the often repeated Challenges of the Missionary would be accepted and he would be silenced.

One hour after Mr. Lockhart arrived the Missionary

forwarded to him a Copy of the Challenges previously
sent, with the following note :—

Boyle, June 11, 1853.

REVEREND SIR,—As you have only to-day arrived here, altho'
announced to have opened your "Mission" upon the 26th of May,
I beg to enclose to you printed copies of the INVITATIONS forwarded to you before this.

Should you feel yourself sufficiently confident in the Truth
of the Creed you now profess, to be able to give us the pleasure
of meeting you as invited, in a PUBLIC DISCUSSION, I shall be
ready, trusting in GOD, and relying on the power of His Word,
"which is Truth," to meet and oppose your newly adopted Creed,
and to defend the Catholic Creed—the Nicene Creed—still professed by me.

Our prayer on your behalf is "that it may please God to bring
into the way of Truth all such as have erred and are deceived."

Your obedient servant,
GEO. W. DALTON, A.B.,
Missionary to Roman Catholics and Vicar of Kilbryan.
Rev. W. LOCKHART.

No reply or acknowledgment was ever sent. On
Sunday morning several of the Protestants received thro'
the Post a printed copy of an address from Mr. Lockhart.
Part of which was a challenge to answer certain questions—and the other part was a reply to an answer he
had elsewhere received. We give the Challenge contained
in the first part of the letter :—

A few words from Father LOCKHART, late B.A. of Oxford, now
Missionary Priest of the Catholic Church, to the Ministers
and Lay Members of the Protestant Church in Ireland :

Having refused several challenges to public controversial discussions, it has been pretty widely stated in newspapers and other
publications, of late, that I, a convert to the Catholic religion and
missionary priest of the same church, am unable or unwilling to
give a reason for my faith. It is perfectly true that I have refused
these challenges—twenty of them at the very least within the
last nine months ; and in this course I shall certainly persevere ;
for having examined the history of the principal controversial
discussions held in this country, I have observed that such modes
of conducting religious inquiry never lead to any conclusion, but
leave the matter much as it was before, both Catholics and Protestants notoriously claiming the victory, the only fruit being an
increase of religious bigotry and party spirit.

However, for those who are uncertain there are other ways of arriving at truth beside public discussion; the means, for instance, which I took myself, and which, as being certainly unexceptionable, I would earnestly recommend to all sincere Protestants, such as I hope I was myself some ten years ago; and the means I would recommend are—

1st—Earnest prayer for light to know the truth, and grace to follow the truth when known.

2nd—A careful examination of what can be said on *both sides of the question*, beginning first by testing Protestantism on its own merits; and ascertaining whether from the Bible and the Bible only, all things can be proved which are essential to Christianity.

I say, then, that I am a Catholic by the grace of God, because I was led to see that some authority, besides the Bible, and the Bible only, was necessary in order to prove many of the very points which all Protestants admit to be essential to Christianity. Protestants deny this, and declare that nothing is necessary to be believed but what can be proved from the Bible and the Bible only—namely, from plain texts of Scripture. The whole question is, therefore, reduced into a nutshell; in the proof or disproof of this, lies the proof or disproof of Protestantism. I do, therefore, solemnly Challenge the Protestants of Ireland to prove by plain texts of Scripture the questions concerning the obligation of

I.—The Christian Sabbath.—1st. That Christians may work on Saturday, the old seventh day. 2nd. That they are bound to keep holy the first day, namely Sunday. 3rd. That they are not bound to keep holy the seventh day also.

II.—The necessity of infant baptism, or any command or permission to confer it.

III.—The canonicity and inspiration of the different books of the New Testament.

If these, or any of these, cannot be proved from the Bible and the Bible only, without reference to authority or tradition, (which latter, according to the principles of Protestantism, is a mere human and fallible guide), I would ask any candid Protestant to say why he believes them still? and if he is determined to believe them in common with Catholic Christians, how does he reject the only ground on which Catholics believe them—namely, the ever living, infallible guidance, promised by our Lord to his Church before a single syllable of the New Testament was written, on the authority of the church of the living God, the pillar and foundation of the truth? (1 Tim. iii. 15: Matt. xxviii. 16—20.)

To this letter the following reply was sent by the Vicar of the Parish :—

REVEREND SIR.—I avow myself as one of those clergymen of the Church of Ireland, who have invited you to a " Public Controversial Discussion". This I most certainly should not have done, had I been aware, that it was your fixed determination not to come forward on such occasions. It is unnecessary for me to say, that you are quite competent to make choice of that course which in your judgment may best promote the interests of the Church of which you are a minister; and I have no disposition to impute to you, on this account, any want of ability or zeal to defend your position. Permit me only to observe, that when any controversialist acts upon this ground, he ought to adopt a studied moderation of tone, both in his statement of facts and reference to individuals. He who claims the privilege of declining to stand on the defensive ought to be restrained, by the very remembrance of this privilege, from wounding an opponent whom he has deprived of all opportunity of retaliation.

I readily admit, that controversial discussions have often produced "Religious bigotry and party spirit"—sad and lamentable evils which form the plague spots of Ireland; but if conducted in a proper spirit, and under wise restrictions, I make no doubt that they would be less likely to lead to this result, than loose assertions and bitter personalities, not very appropriate to the Lord's Day and a Holy place, and I may add, not very edifying to a flock not in danger of sinning by an excess of moderation.

The object which we propose to ourselves is the same, namely the attainment of the truth; we differ as to what it is, and as to the means by which it is to be acquired. I fully coincide in your recommendation of the two means of arriving at the truth, specified by you, namely, 1 " Earnest prayer for light to know the truth, and grace to follow the truth when known; and 2d., a careful examination of what can be said on both sides of the question." But here suffer me to observe, that there are certain conditions, without which we cannot expect prayer to be acceptable before God, among which I would especially call your attention to that mentioned, I. Tim. ii. 8, " I will therefore that men pray in every place, lifting up pure hands *without wrath or contention.*"—(Douay Bible). "As to a careful examination of what can be said on both sides of the question"—I very much doubt whether such a course would be approved of, or permitted by any Irish Roman Catholic Priest unless he differs widely from those with whom I have been acquainted. I have heard language from your colleague, Rev. Father Rinolfi, of quite an opposite tendency, and I make little doubt but that your own *spoken* discourses are rather at variance with this *written* recommendation.

You state that Protestants declare " That nothing is necessary to be believed, but what can be proved from the Bible and the Bible only—namely from plain texts of Scripture." Permit me respectfully to observe, that if you meant to refer to the Church of Ireland, which I believe you did, you have not correctly represented her teaching upon this subject. The 6th Article as you probably may remember upon being thus reminded, declares, "Holy Scripture containeth all things necessary to salvation, so that whatever is not read therein, nor may be proved thereby is not to be required of any man, *that it should be believed as an article of the faith, or be thought requisite or necessary to salvation.*" From this it appears plainly that your statement of her principles is not correct; you say she teaches that "nothing is necessary to be believed, but what can be proved from the Bible;" what she does state is, that "nothing is to be believed as an article of the faith, or be thought necessary to salvation, unless contained in it, or capable of being proved from it."

It is quite superfluous to prove, that many things are to be believed as true, which yet could not be reckoned among the articles of the Christian faith, without the belief of which none can be saved. Unless then you can produce some one of these articles, always recognised and received as such in the Catholic Church, and that it is made to appear there is no authority for it in the Scripture, your exception is of no real force, and does not apply. Every member of the Church of Ireland will readily admit, that she follows many usages of which she can only say, that they are sanctioned by the practice of the Primitive Church, and not opposed to the word of God; but none of them are imposed as necessary to salvation, or as articles of faith.

With this important distinction before our view, I proceed to the consideration of what I may call *your theological puzzles,* which, I may add, the regulations of a well ordered conference would preclude you from producing, so long as you presented yourself in the character of a Roman Catholic Priest. You require me to prove from Scripture, "1st. That Christians may work on Saturday, the old seventh day; 2nd. That they are bound to keep holy the first day, namely Sunday; 3d That they are not bound to keep holy the "seventh day also."—To which I might reasonably reply, are these particulars, articles of the faith necessary to salvation? If not, I am not bound by the rules of the church of Ireland, to prove them from Scripture;—you cannot assert that they are, for it is taught by the divines of the church of Rome that Apostolical tradition is not by itself a rule of faith, and the observance of the Lord's Day is set down as received from Apostolical Tradition. But I consider that the usage of St. Paul and St. John, as mentioned Acts xx, 7, 1 Cor. xvi. 2, Rev. i, 10, quite sufficient warrant and authority for the transfer of the Sabbath from the Seventh to the First Day, and the observance of it as a day of rest and religious exercises, coupled with the direction of St Paul, 1. Cor. xi. 1., "Be ye followers of me, as I also am of Christ."—As to the lawfulness of working on the Jewish Sabbath, I can adduce no direct text such as you require, but the church of Ireland may belter herself under the rule laid down by St. Augustine, "In these things whereof the Scripture appointeth no certainty, the use of the people of God, or the ordinances of our Fathers must serve us for a law."

In reference to your demand for proof from Scripture for "the necessity of Infant Baptism, or any command or permission to confer it," I would reply that the necessity of it is set forth in John iii. 5., "Amen, Amen, I say to thee, unless a man be born again of water and the Holy Ghost, he cannot enter the Kingdom of God."—(Douay Bible). I need hardly remind you that in the original Greek, the word here translated 'a man' signifies a 'person of any age or condition'. The command to confer it, you may find in Mat. xxviii. 18, 19, "Jesus coming spoke to them, saying : all power is given to me in heaven and in earth. Going therefore teach ye all nations : baptizing them in the name of the Father, and of the Son, and of the Holy Ghost."—(Douay Bible). If you object that this command applies only to adults, I would reply, that any promise made by God,—who is declared to be good unto all and rich in mercy,—must be taken in its *widest* sense, and cannot be limited, unless where He does so in *express terms.* The burthen of proving its limitation rests upon the objector ; until this is done, the simple words of the command warrant its universal application. (3.) You call for the proof from Scripture of "the canonicity and inspiration of the different books of the New Testament ;" I answer, neither of these subjects is proposed as an Article of the faith, and as necessary to salvation. It is true that none can be saved without receiving the truths contained in the New Testament ; and yet one might and often does believe the gospel without ever having heard of the existence of some of the books of which it is composed. Unless then you can prove, that it is one of the articles of the christian faith without which none can be saved,—that the New Testament must consist of so many books, neither more nor less,—and propose a theory of inspiration to be received under the same penalty, your objection, as it regards the Church of Ireland, is simply trifling. But even waiving this point, I would observe, that a gainsayer might object to any proof drawn merely from a document whose authority is required to be proved. When our Blessed Saviour was upon earth, He declared in John v, 31, "If I bear witness of myself my witness is not true," meaning that His unsupported testimony to His own claims as the Christ would not suffice to establish them as true ; and further refers to the testimony of St. John the Baptist, to the miracles that He wrought, and to the Holy Scriptures of the Old Testament. There is no doubt, but that they, who were induced, by these attestations to His character, to become His followers, received a fuller and deeper conviction that He was the Son of God from what they saw and heard in His company, than they did from this outward evidence.

In the same manner, the precise number of books recognised as forming the canon of the New Testament is delivered as such by the tradition of the Universal Church. These same books are declared by a succession of writers to be inspired.— The prophecies contained in them, the miracles wrought by the authors of these books or in confirmation of the doctrine contained in them, the martyrdom of so many thousands of every age and condition who thereby attested the sincerity of their belief in them, the holiness of Christ and His apostles, the sublimity of the doctrine and its agreement with that of the Old Testament, confirm to each man's own soul, the character given of them by the church. These considerations, I think it right to add, have been taken from Roman Catholic writers, and were used by them for the establishment of the inspiration and authority of the New Testament.

You may perhaps here object, that the Protestant receives the Scriptures upon only probable grounds ; and that we cannot reach the certainty which the Roman Catholic attains from his belief in the Infallibility of his church,—to which I reply, that universal testimony of friends and enemies in different parts of the world, and, with few exceptions, *unvarying*, forms, a much stronger foundation of faith, than the probable grounds adduced in proof of the Infallibility of the Church of Rome. Let me remind you of the statement made by Mr. Newman, not only that " the seat of *this infallibility is yet undeveloped*, but also that it may be called " probable." Nothing more than this seems to be claimed for it by him, and with this limitation I am ready to avow my belief, that the attestation given by the universal church to the canon of Scripture is probably infallible, that it is such as no national church or private person could with safety reject.

No comparison can be possibly instituted between the evidence from the voice of the church with respect to the Holy Scripture, and that brought forward to support the doctrine of Infallibility, which is spoken of by some modern Romanist advocates, rather as a theory than as a fully established fact,—to which I may add, that Infallibility is more loudly asserted in the writings and discourses of individual Romanists than in the formal creeds or authorized formularies of the church, insomuch that no decisive and clear declaration to this effect can be produced from that source.

Not to err seems to be the attribute of God alone ; to err and to repent is the highest perfection of man. You have committed a grievous error in separating from the church in which God by His Providence placed you; this error you still repeat by the unhappy career you now pursue; but the way of repentance is still open. Let me express my earnest hope, that an increased measure of wisdom from the Father of Lights, a fuller acquaintance with God's holy word, and a closer view of the true character of Romanism, which you may at a distance have contemplated under an ideal form, may restore you to a better state of mind, and lead you to retrace your footsteps.

I am, Reverend Sir,
Your very humble servant,
JOHN M. MAGUIRE,
Vicar of Boyle, &c.
Boyle, June 21st, 1853.

Rev. W. Lockhart.

Amongst the Lay Members of the Church of Ireland who received Mr. Lockhart's letter, was Captain Robertson, who penned the following—a reply which will shew that the ' Scriptures make one wise and thoroughly furnished.'

TO THE REV. W. J. LOCKHART.

Boyle, 17th June, 1853.

Rev. Sir,—I beg to acknowledge the receipt of your printed circular address, forwarded to me thro' the Post-office; and tho' you have left the neighbourhood, yet I consider it a duty to state publicly the suggestions which such a document produced on my mind, as the address has received all the publicity you could give it.

You commence by expressing your strong disinclination to controversy. This I am not surprised at, as you have everything to fear and nothing to hope for from public discussion; and yet, if it be incumbent on any man to assign " a reason of the hope that is in him," it surely must be one circumstanced as you are; who being formerly a member of the Church of England and now a Roman Catholic Priest, ought to be able to give valid reasons for your own change of opinion, by defending your present communion, and proving the unsoundness of your former one, before you invite any one to follow your example.

Had you passed into retirement or obscurity on changing your faith, it would be unseemly to intrude upon your privacy; but having assumed the office of a missionary in propagating your present faith, and as you are compassing sea and land to make proselytes, it ceases to be optional with you to decline controversial discussions. Consistency of character requires it in yourself; deference to public opinion on an important question equally demands it from you. I ask, has there not been one among the twenty challenges which you have received during the last nine months, that you could venture to accept? Is there no one point that you can meet your assailants on? Can an Oxford B.A. a Roman Catholic Priest, a propagandist Missionary, &c. find no arguments to assail a church, acknowledged by himself to *rest on the Holy Scriptues alone,* from which he has separated; or to defend another church unscriptural to his heart's content, which he has joined? If the truth be on your side what have you to apprehend? If your faith be as unquestionable as your zeal, why do you quail before your challengers, or attempt to excuse yourself from a great duty in "contending for the faith once delivered to the Saints" on the feeble and unsatisfactory grounds which you have alleged.

Many perhaps may be entrapped by the subtlety which you have used in directing *"Sincere Protestants"* to the means which you state you adopted in arriving at the truth, (as you call the Romish Faith). These are two-fold,—earnest prayer for Divine grace, &c., and a careful examination of both sides of the question, &c., by the Bible.

I will venture to pledge myself that in your search after Romanism, you did not confine yourself to earnest prayer thro' the one Mediator, and the study of the Bible; for if you had, you would not now be a Romish Priest: and it is a fraud to say that earnest prayer for Divine Grace, and the reading of the Holy Scriptures, ever led you from the Church of England to Romanism. We assert that those peculiar Romish Doctrines which Protestants repudiated at the Reformation, are not to be found in the Bible. We separated from the Romish Church because we proved them to be the Doctrines of men, and we are prepared to prove them so again. We fearlessly assert that they are not only without the authority of Scripture, but that they sprung up many centuries after the times of our Lord and his inspired Apostles; and that the Church of Rome has no authority for her novelties, but the Church of Rome herself. Our Lord says "if I bear witness of myself my witness is not true"; * * * "the Father himself which hath sent me, hath borne witness of me."—John v, 31, 37. Can the Church of Rome, then, suppose that we will receive her testimony of those new doctrines, for which no Divine sanction can be affirmed, and which Ecclesiastical History proves to be spurious and novel.

You call upon us to prove the Change of the Sabbath, the necessity, &c., of Infant Baptism, and the canonicity of the New Testament from the Holy Scriptures, and imply that the absence of Scripture proof on these points, has led you to your present opinions.

It would be an easy matter to give you all the Scripture authority for the Change of the Sabbath, and Infant Baptism, which the Holy Scriptures contain on those two points, and which appears to have been sufficient to induce all the Apostolic Churches to have adopted them, long before the new faith of the Romish Church came into existence; and it would be also easy to prove, that all the Gospels and Epistles of the New Testament were professedly written by the inspired followers of our Lord, and that

C

they bear ample internal evidence of authenticity and inspiration, even without the concurrent testimony of antiquity ; so that the *onus probandi* lies on a Romish Priest to disprove and object to their sufficiency for all matters of *doctine faith and practice*, (II Tim. iii, 16,) as it does to question their very canonicity.

But it is unnecessary to furnish you with the several passages in the Holy Scriptures which refer to these subjects, as I am persuaded you do not require them ; the Rev. Mr. Fowler's letter, and other similar letters which you have doubtless received, have supplied them, if really you desire to make a profitable use of them. But let us see how the case now stands :—As a Roman Catholic Priest you have asked Protestants for such a measure of Scripture proof on certain points, as to satisfy obstinate incredulity, which nevertheless Protestants and Roman Catholics have alway admitted and agreed on. And yet before your change of sentiments, and when you were a member of the Church of England, you did not demand of the Romish Communion Scripture proof for the Invocation of Saints, and Angels, the Adoration of the Virgin, the bowing down and reverence of images and relics, Extreme Unction, Pilgrimages, Penances, Transubstantiation, Purgatory, Rosriaes, and all the other additions made since Apostolic days ; but chiefly for that great and radical error of your whole religion, the doctrine of Justification by Works before God, instead of that precious and soul-saving truth of the Holy Scriptures that a man is justified by faith only in the sight of God through the all atoning merits of the Blessed Saviour. What answer can you give to God or man, when you demand of us Scripture proof for the change of the Sabbath, &c., and have asked none for yourself when embracing such a mass of novelties as you have received on becoming a Roman Catholic? If Scripture proof be necessary for the change of Sabbath and practice of Infant Baptism, how can you dispense with it in matters of such moment as are at issue between the two churches? It must be admitted that the Communion which rests on the entire Holy Scriptures alone, must undoubtedly be right, if she have rightly understood those scriptures ; whilst the Communion, which, in addition to portions of Scripture, rests on Traditions, General Councils, Popes, &c., &c., has so much alloy with the gold, so much sand for its foundation, as to justify the fears of the many who are now anxious to come out of her. But when we examine those sacred Scriptures and see the portrait of the Church of Rome delineated in those Divine pages, we entertain no doubt as to the final issue of the present controversy, or the fearful doom of that unscriptural church.

I remain, Sir, your most obedient servant,

C. ROBERTSON.

Rev. W. J. Lockhart.

The careful Reader will perceive how completely the

Challenge of Mr. Lockhart is demolished by the Rev. J. Maguire, by simply exposing the falsity upon which the former grounded his argument ; and in the letter which so happily comes from the head and heart of a layman—the second reply published—the contrast between the Scriptural support the one creed has, and the total want of the *same* support for the creed of Rome, is well and truthfully put. Surely our Romanist friends must feel it worthy of deepest consideration—how is it that Laity and Clergy alike find the Holy Scriptures the same whence they can meet, attack and refute the Creed of the Church of the Pope of Italy. Can Christ's promise fail ? If the Church of Rome were the Church of Christ and thus preserved on the rock—Christ—she could not, and would not suffer such defeats *every time* that Laic or Cleric assails her with the word of God. Christ's Word could not overthrow his own doctrines. His Church must teach his own doctrines. Christ's Words do overthrow the peculiar doctrines of Rome. Hence we see that the Church of Rome is not the Church of Christ. May our Countrymen feel the bondage they are under.

But to return to the facts of the Mission.—

On Sunday morning, June 12th, Mr. Lockhart addressed the crowds, assembled from 20 neighbouring parishes ; doubtless it was an uncommon sight to see for themselves an Englishman—a reputed learned man—one from Oxford—a convert to the creed, now so strongly and indefensibly assailed out of Scripture and with good reasonings.

The morning's discourse was devoted to false representations of the persecuting spirit of Protestant England. From a demagogue—a political agitator, we would not wonder to hear such garbled statements—such inaccurate historical references—such glaring assertions ; but from a professing Minister of Christ, and one also who had not long FOUND, as he would say, the true Church of Christ, such a discourse was the plainest indication that no solemn—soul-engaging—spiritual motives had led to the

change of Creed. The heart that could give out such
malevolent pictures of England's Protestantism was not
the heart of a Christian. In the course of his address
Mr. Lockhart announced that he would, in the Evening,
give his "Reason" for joining the Church of Rome—
pledging himself not to utter anything offensive to Protestants.

Anxious to hear from his own lips the Reasons which
could induce him to abandon the Church of England, and
desirous of manifesting to the Romanists that they were
ready to hear and to "try" each side, a large body of
Protestants went to the Roman Catholic Chapel on the
Evening of Sunday, June 12. The Missionary also,
under a sense of duty, went to the Chapel. A small sum
of money was expected from all who could afford it, and
was paid before entering the doors. As soon as the
Chapel was filled, it was announced that the Sermon
would be preached in the adjoining field. The whole
mass of the people moved into it. Mr. Lockhart was
raised up on a platform, and opposite to him on a gentle
rise of the ground, on the outskirt of the crowd, the
Missionary, one of the Agents, and a few Protestants,
took their places to listen; and certainly a more painful
exhibition was never by them witnessed—or a more pal-
pable failure manifested. Mr. Lockhart launched forth
into a strain of gross, low abuse—directed against the
Church of Ireland. He endeavoured to shew that no
movement at all existed among the Romanist population—
that the Reformation cry was a " humbug,"—accounting
for it, as a thing got up to stem the outcry which was
raising in England against the Established Church, as a
"humbug" and useless thing. He said that " all the ac-
counts sent across to England of the desire for Protestantism, on the part of the people of Ireland, was mere
puffing—low—disgraceful puffing—like the Newspaper
puffings of Holloway's Pills and Rowland's Macassar
Oil." He furiously denounced all the Clergy of the Established Church—speaking of them, and emphatically of
those connected with the Missionary work now progres-

sing throughout Ireland, as " infernal liars—infernal ruf-
fians—villans,"—saying of them " those white cravatted
parsons are infernal liars,"—" I can't call them anything
else—I would scoff and scorn, and hoot them out." Such
was the sad ebullition of malevolent feeling he gave way
to. Such was the style of argument by which the tottering system of Rome was to be upheld. He made a
sweeping accusation against the character of every convert from amongst the Students or Priesthood of May-
nooth—asserting in vehement terms that " not one of
them had a moral character before they went over—not
one of them would not have been *drummed* out of their (the
Romish) Communion ;" whereas he stood immaculate—
" He had been in Oxford, and not a finger could be laid
on any stain in his character."

Returning from this disgusting self-praise, Mr. Lockhart with other exciting words, as before, boasted of the
change he had made. His " Reasons" for which at last were
about being ennunciated. He stated that on looking into
a Catholic Bible he read the promise of Christ in the last
chapter of St. Matthew, and the 20th verse—" Lo I am
with you always even unto the end of the world." He
argued with himself—the Apostles died—they must have
successors to whom this promise can apply—where are
they ? If he asked the Church of England, they claimed
it not—and here, in fearful daring, he mocked the blessed
truth declared by St. Paul to the Phillipian Jailer—and
said he would be put off by that Church with—Oh !
' Believe and you will be saved.' Don't ask us for the ful-
filment of this promise. If you want that you must go
to the Church of Rome. And so consequently finding
that no Church *claimed* to have the " Umpire" in doctrine
and truth, but the Church of Rome, he joined it. Here
at last his " reasons" were given. Because Rome *claimed*
Infallibility, therefore she possessed it, and therefore he
joined her. When Mr. Lockhart was giving his " reasons"
the Missionary put them upon paper—as surely he should
not forget them, if they were made useful to one soul's
conversion—The crowd greatly excited during the violent

abusive harangue, and roused by the pointed allusions to the "Proselytizing Parsons," and reference to his work and presence, at last dashed at the Missionary, with the design of driving him out of the field, if not of cutting short his existence. The Band of Protestants nobly rallied round the Missionary, and thus protected him from the murderous attack of the mob. As soon as Mr. Lockhart saw the commotion, waving his hand he said—"That's some of the Jumping Parsons wanting to get up a row, and not to mind them." Then becoming excited he shouted—"Put them out," and the efforts of the mob were tremendous to get the Missionary into a hollow in the centre of the field, where humanly speaking he must have been crushed to death. Some of the Police present at once placed the Missionary between them, and aided by the courageous Protestants—few but firm—they succeeded in keeping their footing on the hill and at last getting under safe cover. Two Roman Catholics nobly strove to the utmost to protect the life of one against whom Mr. Lockhart, their Champion, had so roused the passions of the people; who thro' a gracious interposition of God's care, utterly failed in hurting or injuring the object of their hatred. On the return of the mob from the assault, Mr. Lockhart coolly told them he had said the Rosary for them during their absence (at the attack), and that the Blessed Virgin Mary had heard his prayer, and brought them safe back to hear him.

The same mob subsequently attacked the Scripture Readers, and but for the extraordinary courage and efforts of three of the Revenue and Constabulary, they would have taken their lives in the streets.

Such has been the visit and the result of it. Such was the effort of the Church of Rome and the fruits thereof.

On the Monday evening following a riotous mob paraded the streets—shouting for the Readers and Missionary to be brought out and burned, and attacking and smashing the windows of the Mission Lecture Rooms and Readers' Lodgings.

Mr. Lockhart did not appear again, and early on Tuesday morning quietly slipped away from the town.

The Magistrates and Police had to patrol the town the next evening, which prevented an anticipated attack upon the Class-Meeting.

The following observations appeared in the *Roscommon and Leitrim Gazette*, upon Mr. Lockhart's Sermon :

We are just reminded of Mr. Lockhart's hard heartedness since his jump to Rome. What did he say of his PARENTS *here* ?

What did he say of his parents at Newry ?

What did he say of his parents at Clifden ?

Listen! ye who have a heart to feel still strong in its power the love we ever owe to a father, and should feel toward her who in sorrow gave us life, and thro' weal and woe, nights and days, in anxiety and in joy, first taught our lips to frame itself to utter indearing accents—first showed us how to welcome our father—first helped our tottering footsteps, and who, thro' boyhood and thro' youth, watched with deeply feeling and joyous pride, our progress into and acceptance amongst the busy mass of our fellow man. Listen ye to the language, and note ye the hard heartedness of Rome's applauded convert! Did none of you hear him tell you "his parents are in hell" because they died Protestants? And did those lips utter such words! Oh! could thy heart allow it! would not thy brain reel and thy heart faint, Lockhart! ere thou couldst tell a crowd of strangers "thy parents are in hell!" Thank God *our* religion does not stifle our affections! But what saidest thou in Clifden? The same! The son told the peasants of Connemara that his father was burning in hell because he died a Protestant! It is easy work to him to say it, it has been so often said ! But we track thee to Newry—close on the confines of the Protestant North—and what sayest thou THERE? Oh happy announcement for the Protestants of the north, thy father had been burning in hell but now he was *rescued* by you and delivered into HEAVEN!!

Now when in Boyle many heard the statement that the parent was in hell !!!

Which are we to believe? That the parent fell back again ! or another has died, and is not yet—until the neighbourhood of some very Protestant place is visited—to be rescued! Judge ye yourselves people! Who would believe anything from such a man !!

The reference to the "*parent being in hell*" will horrify all who read it—as it did those who heard it.—

In fact, this seemed to arrest attention more than anything else of the painfully wretched effusion he uttered.

The feelings of detestation of the Protestants in consequence of the brutal attack of the mob, yielding to the impulse originated by the brutal language indulged in, were manifested in several letters which appeared in the Paper. And at the conclusion of the usual Controversial Class Meeting on Tuesday evening, the 28th of June, the friends of the Mission to Roman Catholics were requested to remain, it having been decided upon to take that opportunity of presenting an address to the Missionary, which was accordingly placed in the hands of Captain Robertson to read and present, who spoke nearly as follows, as reported in the *Roscommon Gazette*:—

Sir,—I am deputed to present this address to you, arising out of the late dreadful and unprovoked attack made on you, by a very large number of Roman Catholics assembled for the celebration of public worship; but I trust you will not impute to arrogance on my part, my undertaking the presentation of this address, but to the partiality of a friend, who would take no excuse and whom I could not refuse. However, my reluctance has not arisen from indifference or want of sympathy with you on that occasion; no, on the contrary, I fully appreciate your dangerous and arduous duties; and now that I have undertaken this task, I will do it in the spirit of a true Irishman, with all the veins of my heart. I signed that address with such a vehement satisfaction, that I thought I never did anything in my life with more pleasure; I now present it, with, if possible, increased pleasure; and if there is one thing wanting to make my gratification complete, it would be that I had the thoughtful head, and fervid heart, to devise and indite this address; but that merit justly belongs to another.

It is now about 35 years since first my mind was enlightened with the glorious truths of the gospel of our Lord and Saviour Jesus Christ. I then felt like the woman spoken of in the Gospel, who called together her neighbours, saying "rejoice with me, for I have found the piece of silver, which was lost," I too, endeavoured amongst my neighbours to impart to them the peace comfort and hope, which I myself enjoyed thro' the precious Word of God. The Roman Catholics were early and ardently the object of my labours and prayers. I felt the deepest, and most unceasing interest for them; I think I could lay down my life, if I could be of service to their precious souls (hear, hear). The mode I adopted was the reading and expounding of Divine Truth, but something more than that I now see was required;

their errors and consequent dangers should be pointed out, which, out of a mistaken delicacy, I did not touch on ; besides my efforts were associated with any little exercise of charity I was able to administer myself; and often with the benevolences of a Noble Lady whose name is remembered in the memory of thousands. I now see that my plan was defective, and that the mode adopted by the Irish Church Missions is more Scriptural and effective.

In conclusion Captain R. said,—Sir I did not think there was to be found in the Church of Rome a priest who could be guilty of the conduct of Mr. Lockhart, on the occasion alluded to, or that if there was, there would be found a congregation in all Ireland to commit the outrageous act which our own town was witness to on that evening.

Captain R. then read the address, and in conclusion stated that it was signed by Lord Lorton, a name dear and revered by all who knew him (great cheers), by the Hon. R. King, his son, and Mr. King, his grandson, and also by 150 of the most respectable Protestants in the town and neighbourhood.

The following is the Address above referred to, as also the Reply :—

REVEREND SIR,—We the Undersigned, inhabitants of the Town and neighbourhood of Boyle, desire hereby to offer you our heartfelt congratulations upon the providential deliverance you have experienced from the violence of a portion of the congregation, assembled near the Roman Catholic Chapel, on the afternoon of Sunday, June 12th.

The conduct pursued on this occasion, so wholly opposite, we will not say to the Christian religion, but even to common humanity, forms, if it were needed, an additional proof of the necessity of a special mission, such as that which you have come to fulfil amongst us, to convey to such persons that blessed Gospel, which, while it declares God reconciled to man, combines all men who receive it in the bonds of a holy brotherhood, casting out hatred, and bringing in love.

While we would attribute your safety on this occasion to the gracious care of Almighty God, we look upon it as our bounden duty to express our sense of the energy and courage with which our Protestant brethren who were present, in conjunction with some of the Roman Catholics, interposed themselves for your protection.

We feel bound to declare that you are incapable of acting in such a manner as wantonly to provoke any individual or body of men; and we trust that this will be acknowledged by all the members of the Church of Rome, when the present excitement shall have passed away.

We would further express our sense of the diligence and zeal which you have shewn in the discharge of your duties since your appointment as Missionary to the Roman Catholics within this district, and we earnestly pray that God may give abundant success to your labors.

We are, Rev. Sir,
Very faithfully yours,

[THE SUBSCRIBERS.]

ANSWER:—

DEAR FRIENDS,—The manifestation on your part of kind feeling, has not been wanting since I came amongst you; and this, your united expression of congratulation upon my late providential preservation, brings with it a happy indication of the pleasurable connection which you have suffered to be formed between us.

While I regret the outbreak of evil passions to which some have lately been incited, I cannot but feel truly thankful that you see in it the very reasons which may be urged for a continuance of that special mission to which you have bid God speed.

Apart from all personal considerations, I most highly value your Address, inasmuch as it contains the *record* of the "energy and courage with which our Protestant Brethren who were present interposed themselves for my protection"—a fact to be remembered—an act which is and will be remembered while life is sweet to myself, and its continuance cherished by those who make up to me its measure of earthly happiness. And while I thank you for enabling me and mine to possess this the accredited statement of the genuine kindness of my Protestant friends, I join with you to the full in the sense you entertain of the honorable conduct of some of the Roman Catholics present, contrasted, as it must be, with that of the mass.

Your reference to the manner in which the grace of God may have enabled me to carry on the work, "whereunto" (I trust fruits will yet manifest) "He has called me," is peculiarly gratifying. In telling the Truth, we, by a law of our evil nature, become an enemy in the estimation of the opposers of that Truth. May I ever bear in mind that I must needs take heed to my way; your kind reference magnifies the necessity for this.

Unite dear Friends! Unite with me in recollecting the Especial difficulties a large portion of our fellow-countrymen labor under, before the knowledge of the Love of Jesus is theirs, or the power of the Holy Spirit can be brought to act upon them through the Word of God, 'which by our Gospel is preached unto them.' Unite in special prayer on their behalf.—Unite in special efforts for their welfare—and ye, 'helping together with your

prayers,' shall yet see your desire granted—my mission accomplished—our hearts rejoicing at the salvation of souls, as now together you have refreshed the grateful heart of
    Your unworthy servant, for Christ's sake,

                    GEO. WM. DALTON,
                    Missionary to Roman Catholics.

To the Inhabitants of Boyle, &c.,
    Undersigned to the Address.
                                Boyle, June 28, 1853.

The Viscount Lorton—a Nobleman who has shewn the strongest desire for the advancement of the Mission work, feeling it to be the only efficient remedy for the unhappy condition of Ireland, so long and so deeply enslaved beneath the anti-scriptural creed of the Pope of Rome—having had represented to him the very praiseworthy conduct of the Constabulary and Revenue Police, in defending and preserving the endangered lives of the Missionary and Readers,—manifested his appreciation of what was upright, courageous and prompt in them, by transmitting thro' his Agent a reward of £12 to be distributed as a token of his recognition of their excellent bravery on the occasion. Pleasing thus will ever be some of the recollections of this eventful effort, as made by the Church of Rome to check the enquiry awakened in Boyle and its neighbourhood.

But it will be asked—Has Rome laid no claim to success after such a Mission?

She has; and possessed of the document in which we found that she did so, we give extracts from it, and shall add an incident connected with this boast of success.

In the *Freeman's Journal* of July 2d, 1853, appeared an Address from the Inhabitants of Ballaghaderrin, presented to Mr. Rinolfi, who had proceeded thither from Boyle—the reply contains the following passage—the italics are our own:—

Those poor creatures—*upwards of three hundred*—that in *Boyle* and Ballaghaderreen alone presented themselves to me, *even in the public streets*, begging to be reconciled to holy church, show forcibly enough to every sensible man how truly mean and detestable must be the system of those men that could take advantage of such dire distress to make the Irish people, not Protestants, which they could never expect, but simply hypocrites or unbelievers—for of those that they boast of as converts to Protestantism not one has hitherto been found to have turned even for a moment from the religion of their fathers through conviction; but whilst outwardly complying with the sinful conditions, on which alone some slender relief or temporal advantage was offered to them, they were still clinging in their hearts to their former faith, as they solemnly declared at the foot of God's altar.

This is signed " ANGELO MARIA RINOLFI, Missionary-Apostolic of the Order of Charity."

Now we were daily, almost hourly, out of doors and in the streets of Boyle, during this "Mission," and strange to say we neither ourselves saw any one single individual of the "*three hundred*," nor have we heard any one speak of having seen any single individual of these " three hundred presenting themselves in the public streets to be reconciled to holy church." Of BALLAGH-ADERRIN we absolutely heard nothing, except that a thunder-storm terrified, scattered and disappointed Mr. Rinolfi's field-preaching-audience.

However, upon Sunday morning, June 26, 1853, a person publicly recanted in Boyle Chapel.

The following letter was published, fully exposing the case—the *only case* moreover, of the "*three hundred*" which was heard of:—

THE RECANTING OF A READER.

TO THE EDITOR OF "ROSCOMMON AND LEITRIM GAZETTE."

Boyle, July 1st, 1853.

SIR,—On last Sunday morning, a person was brought forward in the Chapel, professing to be one who was desirous of returning to the Church of Rome, from which he had previously separated. I would not have intruded upon the attention of the public any remarks respecting this recantation, but that the officiating Priest read, at the same time, a letter purporting to be from this restored son of the Church, and making statements which require comment.

The person who wrote the letter, and who recanted, is called I believe Larry Corcoran. He states in the letter imputed to him that he had been offered £36 a-year by the Mission Agents in Ballaghaderrin to induce him to change his religion—in other words, that he was BRIBED.

Now, I beg to lay the facts before the Public, and I challenge contradiction. I quote from the reply sent to me by the Rev. A. Thomas, when I inquired respecting Larry Corcoran's past history :—

He writes that " Larry Corcoran kept a hedge school, (not far from Ballaghaderrin), that he had been visited by the Readers, and he professed to be impressed with their scriptural statements—became an inquirer, and immediately he said all his scholars were taken from him by the Priest; he was reduced to great *destitution*—nearly in rags:—the Scripture-Readers took the wretched man thro' a kind feeling into the Mission-House, where they supported him and instructed him for about a month or more, at *their own expense.*

After many conversations and interviews with this man I got him appointed as a *Probationer*, at 5s. per week. From his wretched condition, and inability to go out from almost total nakedness, I got it raised to 30s. per month. After being with us about two months a countryman told me Corcoran owed him 5s. for whiskey ; I told Corcoran that were he to fall into so great sin as drunkenness it would be fatal to him. In some days after the readers came to me and told me that Corcoran was drunk, and riotous, &c., in the Mission-House ; I instantly *dismissed* him and *turned him out of the Mission-House.*"

Now, Sir, such are the facts of the case.

In compassion he was received into the Mission-House, ragged and starving. He was given just enough to keep him, on the supposition that he was what he professed to be. He became drunken and riotous, and was " *turned out* of the Mission-House" !

Has Rome no better case to get up ! After Father Rinolfi's hard work and exceeding heavy labors in Boyle and Ballaghaderrin, and Mr Lockhart's rousing work, have they not a more creditable result ! Why did the recantation not take place at Ballaghaderrin, where he had left the Church ? Was it because *there* it was known that he was one *dismissed* for drunkenness ?

How will the case of bribery be upheld against the Mission, when Corcoran himself tells us that the Priest took the bread out of his mouth by taking the children from his school, and that he was *on that account* fed and nothing more by those who know the religion and belong to the Church of Christ and not that of the Pope ! I know a little more about this Corcoran. I'll keep it or the future. Meanwhile I rejoice to see how completely Rome has failed—as her Priests feel too keenly. She has failed in her late effort to check the Mission work.

It was not a bad thought to get up a case of recovery, but it is bad that so wretched an attempt was made.

Rome dreads controversy. Rome dreads the Scriptures. Rome dreads the light, and plainly proves in every effort and deed that the Church of Rome understands not the reliance of the true Church of Christ upon His promises, and is ever in terror of losing her people, if they think at all about their soul's salvation.

Your's obliged,

GEO. WM. DALTON.

Missionary to Roman Catholics, &c.

So much for the claim to success on the part of Rome. The very case itself attracts attention to the strange discrepancy between the boast and the FACTS.

We were surprised at the Priests referring to the past, on Sunday morning, July 10th, by reading in Chapel, a letter from Mr. Lockhart,—in consequence of which the Missionary published the following letter, addressed

[TO THE EDITOR OF "ROSCOMMON AND LEITRIM GAZETTE."

Boyle, 15th July, 1853.

DEAR SIR,—My attention has been directed to a letter of Mr. Lockhart's, in the *Freeman's Journal* of the 9th, addressed to Mr. M'Tucker here, which letter was read on last Sunday after Mass in Chapel, by the officiating Priest, conveying a distinct denial of the report of Mr. Lockhart having said that his parents were in hell.

Now I am induced to remark that his *denial* is merely following up the routine these "Missionaries" went thro' in *Clifden*, and other places. At Clifden Mr. Lockhart said, and afterwards denied that he had said, that his parents were in hell. In *Boyle* Mr. Lockhart said, and then denies that he had said, the same.

I am acquainted with persons who were in the field, and heard Mr. Lockhart say that his parent was in hell.

But Mr. Lockhart goes so far as, to say in his letter of the 9th, 'that he *never alluded* to his parents.' Hence there can be no possibility of my informants having *misunderstood* whatever he might otherwise have said about his '*parents*;' but it is plain that, in as much as he says that he '*never alluded*' to them,